ON THE BEAT
Policemen at Work

ON THE BEAT

Policemen at Work

**by Barry Robinson
and Martin J. Dain**

Harcourt, Brace & World, Inc., New York

CRB

Curriculum-Related Books, selected and edited by
the School Department of Harcourt, Brace & World,
are titles of general interest for individual reading.

First edition

Library of Congress Catalog Card Number: 68-13816

Printed in the United States of America

Acknowledgments

The authors wish to thank Deputy Inspector Jack Lustig and the men of the 20th Precinct of the New York City Police Department for their cooperation. We are especially grateful to Patrolmen Henry Buck and Joshua Harris for being so helpful and understanding during the days we spent with them on the beat.

HELPING PEOPLE

When people are in trouble and need help, they often turn to a policeman. Helping people is a policeman's job.

He helps boys and
girls who have gotten
lost.

Grown-ups get lost, too, or sometimes they just don't know how to find a certain street. A policeman can give them directions.

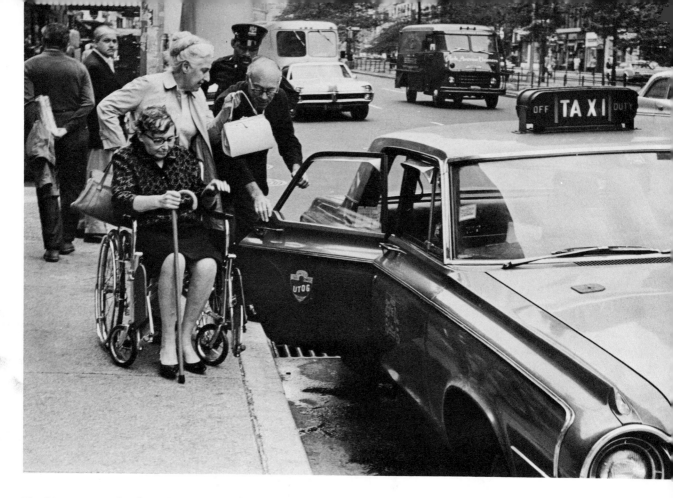

Policemen help sick people and people who have gotten hurt.

A woman who feels faint or dizzy may ask
a policeman to help her home.

A boy who has been hit by a car must be rushed to a doctor. If there is no time to wait for an ambulance, the policeman will put him in a patrol car and, with red roof light flashing and siren wailing, race him to a hospital.

A policeman tries to prevent accidents. He tells children that they should play in safe places instead of on the street near passing cars. He also helps children cross streets on their way to and from school.

Policemen can keep two angry people from fighting by helping them settle their argument.

ENFORCING THE LAW

Laws make it possible for people to live together safely and peacefully. Policemen protect our lives and property by enforcing the laws.

If a car is parked where it shouldn't be, a policeman puts a ticket on its windshield. When the owner returns and finds the ticket, he will have to pay a fine for breaking the parking laws.

Policemen direct traffic and keep cars moving.

A driver who goes faster than the law allows also gets a ticket and has to pay a fine. But in a way he is lucky. If a policeman hadn't stopped him, he might have kept on speeding and crashed into another car.

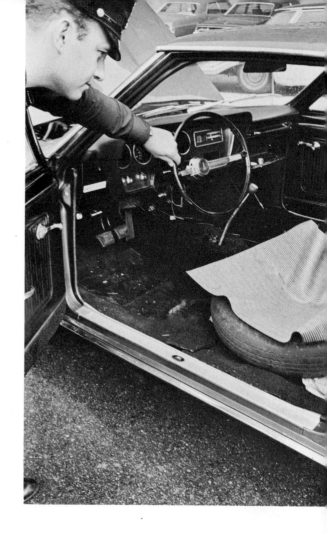

Every policeman carries a list of the license numbers of cars that have been stolen. If he finds a stolen car, he will try to catch the person who drove it away. He will also make sure that the car is returned to its true owner.

While he is walking on his beat, a policeman stops and telephones his stationhouse. The officers at the stationhouse then know where he is and what he is doing. They can send him wherever he is needed. People on the street who want to report crimes in a hurry can use these special phones, too.

Whenever headquarters receives an urgent call it quickly radios a message to patrol cars on the beat. The policemen in the car closest to the scene of the crime speed off to investigate.

Often people report crimes from their own telephones. A woman may call to report that a burglar has broken into her apartment. If the policemen move fast enough, they may catch him.

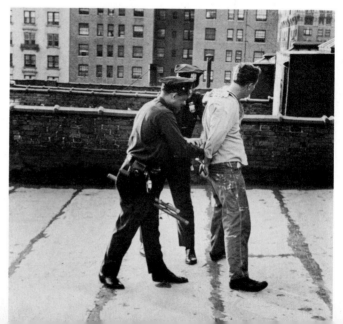

Sometimes policemen are not so lucky, and the burglar has enough time to get away. The policemen must then search for clues that will tell them who he is, where he has gone, and what he has done with the stolen property.

It is very important to have policemen patrolling the streets. People are not likely to break the law when they see a policeman standing nearby. Burglars won't hold up a store or break into a home if they know a policeman is watching.

EARNING A BADGE

A policeman has studied very hard to earn his badge. He has graduated from high school and from the Police Academy. Many policemen keep on studying and attend college during the time when they are off duty.

A policeman has learned about his city and the people in it. He has learned how to give first aid to people who are hurt. He knows the laws he enforces.

He knows how to shoot a gun and handle a night stick. He has practiced judo so that he can defend himself on dark streets and in alleyways without using his gun.

He knows how to use the equipment in patrol cars. Some policemen also can ride a motorcycle or a horse.

He is tall and strong,
with sharp eyesight
and keen hearing.

He is able to think
and move quickly.

When a man has completed his training, he has truly earned the badge of a policeman. He knows how to serve the people of his city.

WORKING FOR THE PEOPLE

Policemen work for us. Our taxes pay their salaries and our votes elect the men who write the laws that policemen enforce.

A good policeman cares about the people he protects, and he is friendly with them.

He likes to see children doing well in school. He also likes to see them having fun! A policeman knows that most happy people do not break the law.

A policeman enjoys chatting with people as he goes about his job.

He talks with shop owners and jokes with a chef in a neighborhood diner.

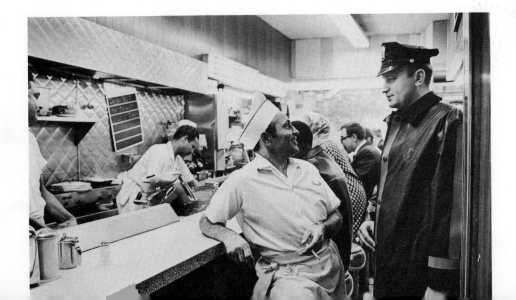

Policemen work hard for us. After being on the beat for nearly eight hours, they must go back to the stationhouse and write up a report of everything important that happened during that time.

After the report is done, a policeman changes from his uniform into his own clothes and takes the subway home. Even when a policeman does not wear his uniform, he always carries his badge and his gun. Many arrests are made by policemen who are off duty.

When policemen are at home, they as well as their families
are among the people being protected. For even while they
rest, other policemen are hard at work.

At every hour of the day and night, policemen are on the beat.